# John Gardner

# Carols

## *11 carols for mixed voices*

MUSIC DEPARTMENT

# OXFORD

UNIVERSITY PRESS

OXFORD
UNIVERSITY PRESS

Great Clarendon Street, Oxford OX2 6DP, England

Oxford University Press is a department of the University of Oxford.
It furthers the University's aim of excellence in research, scholarship,
and education by publishing worldwide

Oxford is a registered trade mark of Oxford University Press
in the UK and in certain other countries

3 5 7 9 10 8 6 4 2

ISBN 978–0–19–338816–1

Music and text origination by
Katie Johnston
Printed in Great Britain on acid-free paper by
Halstan & Co. Ltd, Amersham, Bucks.

# Contents

# Index of Orchestrations

Orchestral accompaniments for the following carols are available to hire from the publisher's hire library or appropriate agent:

*A Gallery Carol*
perc(opt: timp, xyl, glock, tri, tamb, SD, cym), org(from vocal score)

*How bright the Morning Star does shine*
fl(opt), ob, cl(opt), bn, hn, tpt(opt), tbn(opt), timp(opt), str

*O little town of Bethlehem*
2fl, 2ob, 2cl, 2bn, 4hn, 2tpt, 3tbn, tba, timp, perc, hp(opt), str

*The holly and the ivy*
3fl(IIIopt), 3ob(IIIopt), 3cl(IIIopt), 2bn(opt), 4hn(opt), 2tpt(opt), 3tbn(opt), tba(opt), dance band drummer(not essential but highly desirable), pno(opt when full orchestration used), str

*for Neville Atkinson and the Choir of Perse School for Girls, Cambridge*

# A Gallery Carol

## Op. 109 No. 4

Anon.

JOHN GARDNER

When sung by women's or boys' voices only, the soprano and alto parts are taken throughout.

Originally published as the fourth piece in *Four Carols*, Op. 109.

earth! ___ For this ___ is the birth-day of
spy, ___ Pro - claim - ing the birth-day of

Je - sus our King, Who brought us sal - va - tion, his ___ prai - ses we'll sing! ___
Je - sus our King, Who brought us sal - va - tion, his ___

2. A hea-ven - ly ___

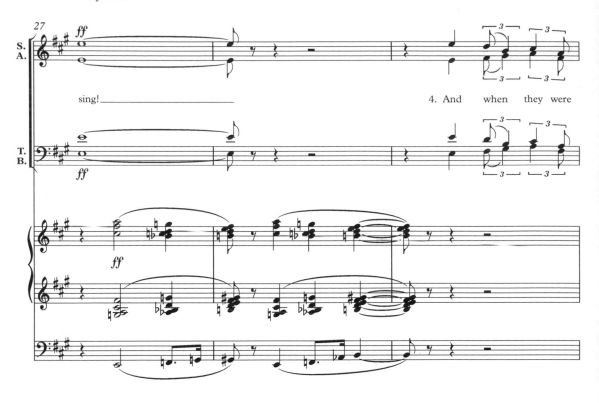

sing!_____   4. And   when   they   were

come, they their trea-sures un - fold,_____   And   un - to him__

of-fered myrrh,  in - cense, and  gold._____  So___

bless - ed  for-ev-er  be  Je - sus  our  King,  Who

brought___ us sal - va - tion, His___ prai - ses___ we'll___

sing!_____

*New Malden, August 1970*

*for Neville Atkinson and the Choir of Perse School for Girls, Cambridge*

# A Christmas Hymn

## Op. 109a

Hymn at First Vespers,
Christmas Day
trans. John Gardner

JOHN GARDNER

When sung by women's or boys' voices only, the soprano part only is taken, dividing into Sopranos I & II in bars 20, 22, 47, 48, 52, 56, and 60 to the end.

Ere you did share your fa-ther's light.____ You are the bright-est lamp in heav'n;
*Pá - ter sup - ré - mus é - di - dit.____ Tu lú-men et splén - dor Pá - tris,____*

You are our ev - er - last - ing____ hope. Hear now what your hum-ble ser - vants
*Tu spes pe-rén - nis óm - ni - um: In - tén - de quas fún-dunt pré - ces____*

Liv-ing on earth do say____ to you. Re-mem-ber, foun-der of all things,____
*Tú - i per órb-em sér - vu-li. Me-mén - to, ré - rum Cón-di-tor,____*

How you be-came but one of us    When is-su-ing from the Vir - gin's_ womb,
*Nós - tri quod ó - lim cór - por - is,    Sa - crá - ta ab ál - vo Vír - gi - nes*

**movendo un poco**

bear pre - sent
*hoc práe - sens*

You took the form of man on earth.    May this day bear    pre-sent wit - ness,
*Na - scén - do, fórm-am súmp - se - ris.    Tes - tá - tur hoc    práe-sens dí - es,*

**movendo un poco**

*for S.P.G.S.*

# Angels, from the realms of glory

## Op. 58 No. 1

J. Montgomery (1771–1854)    JOHN GARDNER

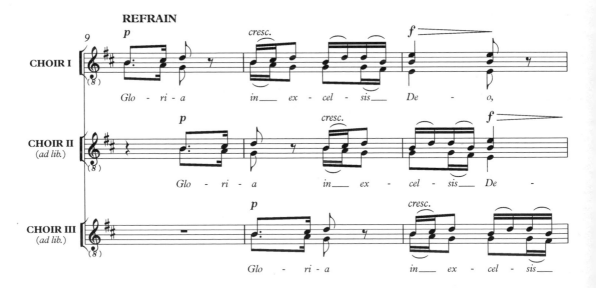

This carol may be sung by equal or mixed voices. The refrain may be sung by one or two choirs only, if preferred. When mixed voices are used the second or third choir of the refrain may be given to men's voices. Alternatively each choir may consist of mixed voices with S doubling T and A doubling B. The conductor should strive to obtain a maximum variety of textures.

*New Malden, October 1963*

*for Neville Atkinson and the Choir of Perse School for Girls, Cambridge*

# Balulalow

## Op. 109 No. 2

attrib. James, John, and Robert Wedderburn (*c.*1567)

JOHN GARDNER

O my dear heart, young Je - sus sweet, Pre - pare thy cra - dle

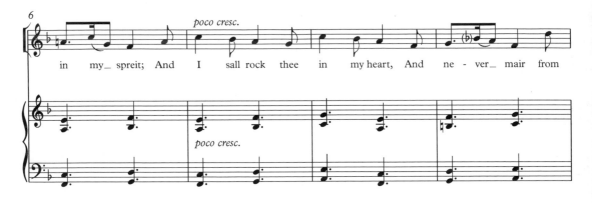

in my_ spreit; And I sall rock thee in my heart, And ne - ver_ mair from

thee de - part. But I sall praise thee ev - er - more, With sang - es sweet un -

When sung by women's or boys' voices only the soprano and alto parts are taken throughout.

Originally published as the second piece in *Four Carols*, Op. 109.

thee de- part. But I sall praise thee ev- er- more, With

sang- es sweet un- to thy gloir; The knees of my heart

sall I bow, And sing that richt ba- lu- la-

*New Malden, August 1970*

*for Louis Halsey and the Elizabethan Singers*

# How bright the Morning Star does shine

## Op. 82 No. 1a

P. Nicolai (1556–1608)
trans. John Gardner

Melody by P. Nicolai
JOHN GARDNER

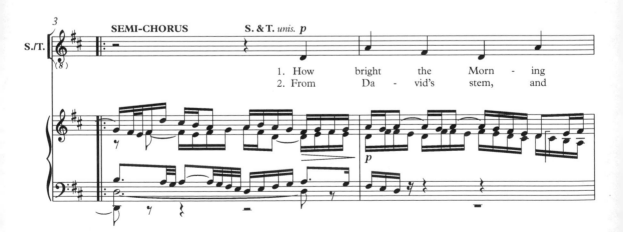

1. How bright the Morn - ing
2. From Da - vid's stem, and

'How bright the Morning Star does shine' was specially adapted from the first movement of *Cantata for Christmas* (Op. 82) for this collection.

*New Malden, October 1966*

*for Will Andress of Shreveport*

# O little town of Bethlehem

## Op. 149 No. 1

Phillips Brooks (1835–93)

JOHN GARDNER

# Sunny Bank Carol

## Op. 141

Trad. English

JOHN GARDNER

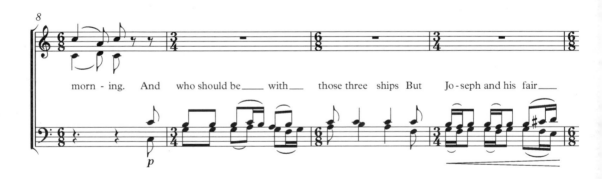

*for S.P.G.S.*

# The holly and the ivy

## Op. 58 No. 2

Trad. English

JOHN GARDNER

Almost any combination of equal or mixed voices, choirs or soloists, may be used in singing this carol. The optional parts for S. & A. in verse 6 should not be given to men's voices, however.
The word 'choir' must be disyllabic always.

Also available separately (ISBN 978–0–19–353154–3).

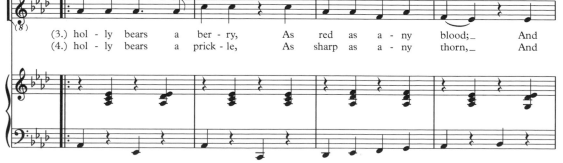

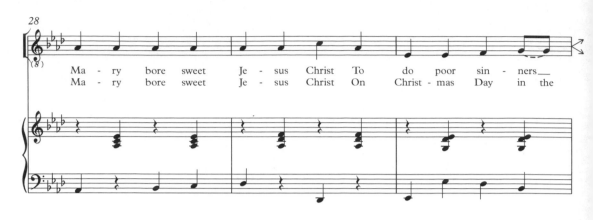

Ma - ry bore sweet Je - sus Christ To do poor sin - ners
Ma - ry bore sweet Je - sus Christ On Christ - mas Day in the

1
good:
morn:  The ris - ing of the sun, And the run - ning of the

2
good:
morn:  The ris - ing of the sun, And the run - ning

deer, The play - ing of the mer - ry or - gan, Sweet sing - ing in the

of the deer, The play - ing of the mer - ry or - gan, Sweet sing - ing

**Verse 6 only: Descant (ad lib.)**

*St Paul's Girls School, October 1963*

# Welcome, Yule!

## Op. 50

Anon. 15th cent.

JOHN GARDNER

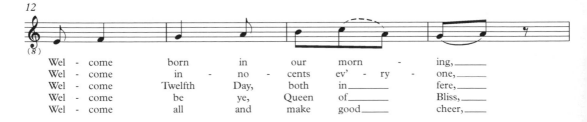

Dynamics may be added at the conductor's discretion.

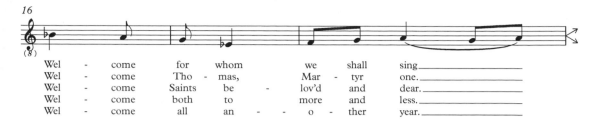

Wel - come for whom we shall sing____
Wel - come Tho - mas, Mar - tyr one.____
Wel - come Saints be - lov'd and dear.____
Wel - come both to more and less.____
Wel - come all an - o - ther year.____

**HIGH VOICE**

*1.–4.* / *5.*

Wel - come, wel - come, wel - come, Yule! Yule!

**LOW VOICE**

Wel - come, wel - come, wel - come, Yule! wel - come,

Wel - come, wel - come, wel - come, wel - come,

wel - come, wel - come, wel - come, wel - come,__

*div.*

wel - come, wel - come, wel - come, Yule!

wel - come, wel - come, wel - come,__ Yule!

*1962*

*for the Springhead Xmas Play, 1950*

# Entry of the Three Kings

\*Matthew 2:1–2

JOHN GARDNER

\*Adapted by John Gardner

† Alternatively, this part can be played on violin or an oboe organ stop. The part is printed separately on p. 64.

*Morden, December 1950*

# We wish you a merry Christmas

Trad. West Country
arr. JOHN GARDNER

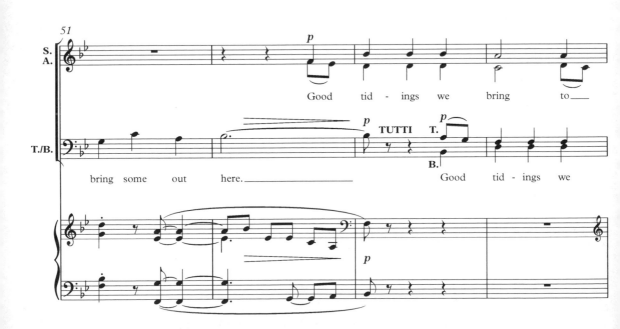

# Entry of the Three Kings

JOHN GARDNER

*Morden, December 1950*

*Alternatively, this part can be played on violin or an oboe organ stop.
†The repeat can be taken once or twice, at the performers' discretion.

This page may be enlarged on a photocopier to facilitate performance.